CONTEMPORARY INTERIORS

BETA-PLUS

CONTEMPORARY INTERIORS
originally published in Dutch and French
HEDENDAAGSE INTERIEURS/INTERIEURS CONTEMPORAINS

PUBLISHER
BETA-PLUS sa
Termuninck 3
7850 Enghien
Belgium
Tel : +32 (0)2 395 90 20
Fax : +32 (0)2 395 90 21
Website: www.betaplus.com
E-mail: betaplus@skynet.be

PHOTOGRAPHY
Jo Pauwels a.o. (photography credits p.216)

LAYOUT
POLYDEM sprl
Nathalie Binart

TRANSLATION
Alexia Aughuet (Dutch to French)
Yvonne Lim and Serena Narain (French to English)

August 2005
ISBN: 907-721-337-6

Left
A bathroom designed by Olivier Dwek.

Next
This kitchen is created by interior designer Nathalie Van Reeth.

SANTOS

CONTENTS

VAN EYCK

PREFACE

In this publication, over 20 renowned architects and interior designers expose their visions of contemporary residence.

These projects are extremely varied in terms of departure point as well as conception: a contemporary residence constructed from an old linen factory, a current renovation of an old master house, a transformation of a sailor's house into a pleasing living and working space, a sober restoration of an authentic hotel, a hyper modern apartment in a contemporary building, etc.

These few articles, however, are based on a same element: the permanent search for the essentials in architecture and interior design.

This quest, in general, drives interior designs that witness a pleasant living minimalism: sober and stripped with respect for the right proportions of warm and natural colours. The timeless quality of materials and the contemporary know-how form the centre of each project.

This is probably what we know as serenity and refinement, which are encompassed in these interiors.

LEFT
A work by Sophie Campion in a house created by architect Baudouin Courtens.

NEXT
This kitchen is designed by interior designer Patric Deknock.

Miele

Chapter I

INSPIRING WORKS

RADICAL TRANSFORMATION OF A 1959 VILLA

Olivier Dwek is a young architect from Brussels who, in a period of four years, has build up a good set of clientele from more than ten interior designs for offices, boutiques and a few private houses.

This article presents Olivier Dwek's recent project in a timbered region in Uccle. A classical 1959 villa is entirely remodelled and transformed. Construction works lasted for two years: several walls were demolished and the spatial layout was entirely changed. The refinement of interior design contributes to the serene atmosphere and the intimacy of the place: the choice is exclusively on high quality warm materials as well as Portuguese natural stone, tinted oak parquet floors, leather and velvet coverings, silk curtains, etc.

All sofas, poufs, low tables, meridian, armchairs, shagreens and benches are designed by architect / interior designer Caroline Notte and realised by famous armchair fabricator from Brussels, Vanhamme.

As a whole, the space breathes a classy contemporary and timeless feel: a work that allows the perception of a promising future for Olivier Dwek.

The monumental entry hall is inspired by the Guggenheim Museum in New York. Sculpture by Tony Cragg.

LEFT
This meridian is designed by Caroline Notte and covered in flamed flex velvet (Donghia) with a coffee tint.

NEXT
In the background, two armchairs in flannelette from Marie's Corner with cushions in anthracite leather in plain flower. To their left, two shagreens in leather. The "long wick" carpet is custom-made in pure wool. An indirect lighting is integrated into the 'floating' ceiling.

The sofa on the left of the photo (almost 4 metres long) is covered in flannelette from Marie's Corner. The bench on the left of the chimney is realised in "China Red" silk velvet. The U-shaped low table overhanging the pouf is in wenge wood.

The open chimney in black cast iron is designed by Claire Bataille. On the foreground, a wax painting by Spanish artist, Jose Maria Sicilia.

ABOVE
The floor of the entry hall is in Portuguese natural stone, Azul Cascais. The curved and bevelled skirting, done by a craftsman, displays the project executor's passion for all details.

The study table for the master of the house and the console, both in tinted oak, are designed by Olivier Dwek. The canvas painting is by Italian painter Flavio Piras.

The game room is lit up by "Icebox" suspended lights by Tal. The photograph is by German artist Andreas Bitesnich. Curtains in silk.

Left

The fully stainless steel laundry inspired by an industrial kitchen style is created by Olivier Dwek. Here too, the choice is made on Portuguese natural stone, Azul Cascais for the floor finish.

de qui
MERCATOR

The staircase and all the flooring for the house are realised in superior quality coloured oak.

Passage to access to the inner portion of the library and to a long space. Suspended ceiling creates an indirect lighting ambience. Primitives sculptures from South Africa.

Left
The monumental library shelf is made-to-measure on two stories with gangway access by Olivier Dwek, in collaboration with Claire Bataille.

Next
The bedroom in a 'Loft' style. The headboard is made up of a curved wall, with access to the bathroom.

CONTEMPORARY RESIDENCE ON THE FOUNDATION OF AN OLD LINEN FACTORY

We owe the construction of this residence resting on the foundation of an old linen factory and situated along Lys to architect Bernard de Clerk.

In the choice of fabrics, interior designer Marc Stellamans looked into the historic context of the masonry: all interior fabrics and carpets in the salon are in linen. All walls and doors are wrapped in coloured fabric.

The choice of materials accentuates the serenity of this house: the ground is in Buxy Gris natural stone; floor in grey French oak; in the rooms, timber works and wall cupboards with brushed plating from Oregon, etc. The kitchen, staircase core, bedrooms and bathrooms are realised by Marc Stellamans.

The purified timeless conception, however, conceals a series of technical equipment: floor heating and air-conditioning systems, as well as a home automation system.

The basin is made of Buxy stone.
Tap is from Vola.

LEFT AND ABOVE
The hall with a symmetrical double staircase is in Buxy natural stone. Wall lights are from Eric Huysmans.

The different spaces are separated by sliding panels.

The bar blends well with the terrace.

LEFT

Flooring in French oak is greyed. On the left, an art work by Miryan Klein; in the background, a painting of Bernar Venet. The custom-made sofa is covered in linen.

NEXT

Kitchen floor and worktop are also in Buxy stone. Custom-made cabinets are in tinted oak. Raffia chairs are from Zanotta.

A detail of the home automation system: switches in steel plates.

Stainless steel handles are custom-made.

LEFT

In the bedroom, Marc Stellamans has chosen brushed timber panels from Oregon, which creates a very warm and intimate ambience.

P.34-35

For the bathroom, the choice is made on France stone, Massangis. Wall panels and cupboards with brushed plating from Oregon.

CONTEMPORARY APARTMENT IN AN OLD BUILDING

Brussels interior design office, M.E.G., lead by Esther Gutmer, has renovated an apartment in a building that dates back to the start of the previous century.

The apartment was initially divided into smaller rooms. It is entirely stripped and bared by Esther Gutmer, who has redistributed the space.

On the left, the painted door is in the same colour as the walls, which conceal behind them the laundry and a study. The custom-made furniture presents an anthracite-lacquered finish. Cooker and hood are from Viking.

The whole wall composition (fridge, stove and drawers) is made of stainless steel.

LEFT
Two sliding doors open into the kitchen with its walls in chalk colour. The floor is in Vinalmont stone and countertop in Corian. The blinds are in light grey linen.

On the foreground on the table is a double plate in oxidised steel and glass (a creation of Esther Gutmer), and a note of old music (Y. David gallery). A Barcelona meridian in maroon leather and carpet in stitched felt. A dining table in wenge wood from Liaigre. Flooring in grey aged oak. A couch in maroon linen from Ralph Lauren. On the grey wall is two paintings by Sophie Cauvin and to the left, a drawing of John Lennon. Curtains are in grey flannel (Ralph Lauren).

The corridor that links the apartment from one part to another is panelled in sanded solid oak and painted white, which accentuates the aspect of the space (a work by general enterprise, 3eme Bureau). Floor is in grey aged oak.

Above

The wall at the head of the bed is painted in dark maroon. The book shelves are in green afrormosia, and so are the two bedside tables (a creation of Esther Gutmer, realised by 3eme Bureau). Two old photos depict New York.

The door, covered in coloured afrormosia, opens into the dressing room that is finished in the same wood.

Bathtub is made of natural stone. Linen blinds are from La Cuona.

LEFT
The basin cabinet is made of wenge wood, chrome and raw schist (creation of Esther Gutmer). The floor is finished in large slabs of softened schist. Tap fittings from Dornbracht are in matt nickel. Framed mirrors conceal two medical cabinets. Wall lights from Liaigre in epoxy.

LEFT
Floor and vanity top are in raw-coloured natural stone. The furniture in oak is coloured in the same tone as the stone. Wall lights from Liaigre.

TIMELESS CLASS AND DISCRETION IN A VILLA

This house, built in 1958 by Brugean architect Vierin in an idyllic surrounding close to a golf course, was recently transformed by interior designer Philip Simoen.

The exterior of this classical villa has not changed; on the contrary, the villa has undergone a true rejuvenation, furnished with furniture pieces that come from the collections of Liaigre, Le Corbusier, Maarten Van Severen, etc and installed in exclusive custom-made elements, sycamore and pear tree wood.

Today, the whole composition of the masonry delivers class and discretion: Simoen's choice for warm and durable materials and his pure style immerse the whole ensemble in a sober and serene atmosphere.

LEFT AND ABOVE

The salon, decorated with an open chimney, is realised by De Puydt (Drongen). On the left of the chimney is a custom-made hi-fi cabinet and on the right is another cabinet that hides the plasma television screen. The coffee table is also made-to-measure. Armchair and bench are by Christian Liaigre; carpet in cotton, silk and linen from Bartholomeus at Torhout.

The sitting furniture is by Christian Liaigre. A wenge wood corner table and a bronze lamp.

View of the dining room from the living room. Base stands are custom-made with two "court ladies" from Gisele Croes gallery at Brussels placed on each stand.

Above

The custom-made cupboards are in pear tree wood. Furniture pieces by Le Corbusier for Cassina.

View of the library from the hall. A serigraphy art work of Lenin by Andy Warhol.

The custom-made kitchen is in European maple wood, an exclusive essence of wood. Worktops are in sanded stainless steel. In the niche above the door on the left is a Multiple de Cesar.

Kitchen floor is in Massangis Roche Claire stone. Cooker and oven from Smeg, and hood is from Gaggenau. On the right foreground is a "Silver" chair by De Padova.

LEFT

Chairs with leather sitting cushions and fabric backrests by Christian Liaigre surround a table from Maarten Van Severen. Curtain fabric from Zimmer & Rohde.

This dressing room is entirely made-to-measure in sycamore wood. The central block of drawers also serves as a folding table. Concealed lighting from Modular; a bench by Christian Liaigre.

The resting room. Dressing room is custom-made with painted frames, glass and curtain nettings. "Mozart" armchair from Flexform. The "Castanza" lamp is by Luceplan.

LEFT

The master bedroom with flooring in oak parquet from Parket Brabo. Bed linen in "Bamboo" fabric from Malabar. Chairs are from Maxal and lamps from Liaigre.

The basins rest on a stainless steel structure. Behind the strips in between the mirrors are the convectors.

"Tara" tap from Dornbracht.

LEFT

The large bathroom is decorated in big Carrara marble slabs. The heater-cum-towel rail is from Barwill.

VAN EYCK

LIGHTING, SYMMETRY AND SOBRIETY

Construction of this contemporary house began after the owners fell in love with one of the last terrains without a view of another building, which is available in a residential area situated at the border of Bois de la Cambre and surrounded by trees that are centuries old.

The project was entrusted to architectural firm Baudouin Courtens. The owners wanted a family house (two children and two dogs) opened towards the exterior, with a priority on lighting, symmetry and sobriety.

The entry hall in Pietra Piasentina marks the rhythm of passage towards all the rooms on the ground floor and to the discrete staircase core that connects the ground level to the mezzanine floor, where the bedroom of the apartment owner is situated. "Lola" wall lights from Liaigre. Two benches in oak.

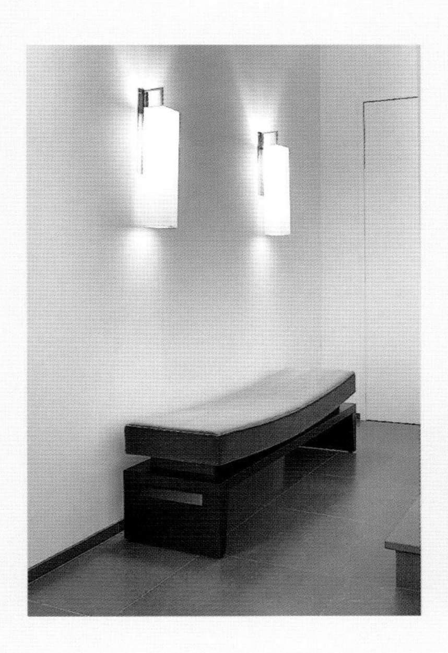

LEFT
The salon at the centre of the house opens towards the hall, dining room and study / entertainment room by high sliding doors in grey brushed oak. The three rooms open into the garden and can be partitioned from one another when necessary.

The linen curtains are identical in the three rooms to mark openness and sobriety. Two Chinese chests of drawers mark the entrance to the dining room. The saffron Souveraine linen of the sofa is highlighted by Jim Thompson silk cushions in a colour between orange and red. The leather pouf is by Christine Liaigre. An Olivier Strebelle's sculpture scoffs at the Yoruba mascot.

NEXT
We enter the living room by two sliding doors in brushed oak that are in the same rhythm as the volume of the ground storey. An angled sofa from Interni. The console in purple wood and steel demarcates the kitchen and office space from the living room. Low cushioned chairs in orange linen and a small Hurel table. An African jar is placed on the coffee table. A Moba – Togo figurine is positioned against the fireplace. African locks are displayed on the console.

The panels in grey oak create a warmer ambience for the dining room. A recessed joint along the entire length of the panel serves as a handle to open the cupboards. The dining table is custom-made, so are the suspended lights. A bowl in brushed sycamore from Ernst Gamperl is seen on the table.

A detail of the panelling. Antelope Bamabara post.

P.58-89
Access to study / entertainment room is announced by the brown olive oak panelling. The warm ambience is marked by the colours of the panels and book shelves. A Hurel sofa with silk cushions from Jim Thompson. A low table in ebony. All the audiovisual equipment is concealed behind a sliding door.

LEFT
A detail of the panelling. Hurel armchair in orange linen and silk from Jim Thompson. On the right is a pouf in smooth velvet.

NEXT
The kitchen is realised by Obumex in grey oak. Flooring and worktop are by Pietra Piasentina. Stools are from Claire Bataille. An Oceanian basket and African jars.

Miele
Miele

Dressing room and bedroom are separated by a pivot panel in tinted brushed oak that disappears and forms part of the U-shaped panelling of the bedroom when it is closed. The central furniture is composed of drawers and covered in leather, just like the bench. All timber sheets are specifically chosen and assembled.

Sophie Campion's mission: to feel and translate what the owners want. A close collaboration that precedes sobriety of materials, warmth of natural base colours, harmony that reins all around the room, and a future room for art pieces. The choice of African art reflects this search for noble and raw materials. Wood is the element of harmony between all the rooms.

LEFT AND RIGHT
The bathroom is hidden behind one of the wall panels in the bedroom. Floor, bathtub and vanity top are in Buxy Cendre. The long furniture piece in tinted oak is in harmony with the stone. Square basins are embedded.

NEXT
The bedroom plays on the view of sunrise. The choice of shades ranges from soft grey (curtains in steamed linen) to beige linen for the bedspread and blinds, and dark brown for the Hurel leather study table and the cushions. The headboard adds extra thickness to the walls and reveals the doors to the dressing room and bathroom.

SONY

MONASTIC AMBIENCE IN A FORESTER'S HOUSE

Interior designer Nathalie Van Reeth has transformed a forester's house into a sober residence with a very relaxed ambience. A portion of the house is finished in cedar wood that was tinted grey; other walls are limewashed.

This house releases a monastic ambience: all the rooms are reduced to the essentials. A place to meditate next to nature, far away from the superficial universe.

An open masonry chimney with restored black stones and Bourgogne pave stone in the foyer separates the open concept living and dining rooms. The bench comes from Ethiopia; books and CDs are arranged on oak shelves. On the floor, a Turkish kelim is seen.

Left
The small hall: walls and balustrade are limewashed in white. The stairs and doors in solid oak are tinted grey.

The kitchen with an appealing view of the woods and the lake. The countertop and sinks are in Moroccan zilliges. A Viking cooker. Handles of the window are in black steel. Tap fittings are from Volevatch.

LEFT

The oak cabinets and flooring in the kitchen are tinted grey. Table and bench in painted pine.

The guest room is finished in hamman. Custom-made basin is finished in lead. Boffi taps, oak shelves.

LEFT
The night hall. Oak floor and frameless pivot doors. A Liaigre lamp. The doors are specially conceived in solid oak for this house.

LEFT
Serene and intimate ambience in the bathroom. Here too, oak flooring is tinted grey. The walls in cement are polished. Ceiling in raw wood is painted white. The bathtub is made of brownish grey sandstone. Tap fittings are from Boffi.

THE SEARCH FOR ULTIMATE SOBRIETY AND PURE BEAUTY

The famous dressmaker Edouard Vermeulen (Natan) has requested architect Vincent Van Duysen to design an apartment in a building realised by architect Marc Corbiau, located 15 minutes from his work place where he can get away to find calm and tranquility.

This huge apartment releases beauty and an almost sacral serenity: a return to the essence of architecture and interior design. All is reduced to its most simplistic expression: the play of simple lines, the perfect symmetry of architecture, the monochromatic palette of white, the force of natural materials, etc. In this residence, each detail reveals Edouard Vermeulen's passion for pure form and his constant search for elegance and beauty.

Opposed to every trivial detail, the architects and owner of the apartment reveal their representation of what constitutes a contemporary residence: a return to serenity and purity in an agitated world.

LEFT AND ABOVE
Edouard Vermeulen found his secondary residence in Brussels in an apartment created by the architects Marc Corbiau and Vincent Van Duysen. On the foreground, a footstool covered in white leather. The oak floor is bleached.

NEXT
Detail of the living room with a meridian by Mies van der Rohe.

Left and Above
Oak flooring is installed in the whole apartment, reinforcing the feel of space and uniformity.

The bronze vase is by one of the protagonists of minimalism, John Pawson.

Next
The bedroom with photos of Stephanie Schneider on the foreground. Lamp from Liaigre.

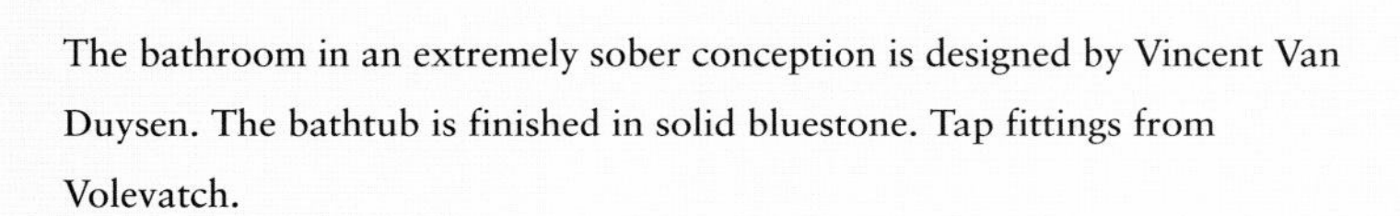

The bathroom in an extremely sober conception is designed by Vincent Van Duysen. The bathtub is finished in solid bluestone. Tap fittings from Volevatch.

CHAPTER II

CONTEMPORARY CLASSICS

HARMONY OF OLD AND NEW

Interior designer Marc Stellamans has transformed a classical 1949 country house into a current and timeless ensemble. The house was entirely restored: an all-new kitchen installed, flooring for the hall replaced, the rooms redistributed, etc. Nonetheless, a number of original elements rest intact: the timber works originally created by the famous French office Jansens is bleached, the existing parquet is re-coated in a dark tint, etc.

The harmonious association of new and old contributes in creating a refined whole, which is pleasant to live in.

In the hall, we discover the Walloon stone of Vinalmont on the floor. The walls are finished in a light sand textured paint. The lustre, a true masterpiece, is by A. Vergara. An art piece by Jan Fabre hangs on the left.

LEFT

The original parquet is conserved and coated in a dark tint. Seats from Flexform; stools in red velvet surround a bar in zinc.

NEXT

Timberworks are realised by Parisian office, Jansens. Marc Stellamans has conserved this original element: only the partitions are bleached. Maxalto seats around a custom-made low table in solid oak. Ceramics are from Tjok Desauvage. Carpet is in linen.

SULTANAS
TEA
SUGAR
CURRANTS

“Cab” chairs from Cassina around an old oak table. All the kitchen appliances are concealed behind pivot and sliding doors. “Tara” tap is from Dornbracht.

LEFT

The kitchen floor is in Vinalmont stone; worktop in steel with custom-made integrated handles.

CONTEMPORARY TRANSFORMATION OF A HISTORICAL HOUSE

"T Schippershuys", a 16th century house and old refuge place for sailors situated at Duurstede (The Netherlands) was transformed by Chris van Eldik and Wendy Jansen into a residence and workplace where new and old confront each other in a fascinating way.

This young couple manages the interior design shop Zon van Duurstede and the brand of furniture, Job. With their own hands, they have transformed this house into an airy and rectilinear whole where their creations are magnificently celebrated with a number of art pieces and learnedly selected old furniture.

The contrast with the original house is surprising!

The office of Chris van Eldik and Wendy Jansen is installed on the mezzanine floor. An old office table is finished in black patina. The bench and armchair are from Job and the artwork is by an artist from Zeist, Beate Emanuel.

LEFT
The linen armchairs that Job created were inspired by old models. The curtains are also in 100% linen. Lamps from Casadisange. An old portrait is placed above the fireplace.

NEXT
The front room on the second storey. On the foreground is an old table in oak. Royal benches and armchairs are arranged around the fireplace. The floor is finished in oak timber.

WONEN MET HOUT
LOFTS OF ANTWERP
AMERICAN COLONIAL

The shelves with an indirect lighting have a hidden fixing detail.

The boudoir, according to a Costermans project.

LEFT

The dressing room in French oak is entirely custom-made according to Costermans' design.
Lighting is by Stephane Davidts. Floor finish in French oak is in the same colour as the cupboards.

A SOBER COASTAL APARTMENT WITH MARITIME ACCENTS

A 140-square metre apartment situated at the sea damn in Knokke is designed by Sand's Company. Carcass works are carried out by architectural office Demyttenaere.

This holiday residence is conceived in a sober and contemporary style, with some maritime accents. All the walls are white and the apartment opens largely out to the sea, which confers an intense sentiment of space.

The apartment consists of three bedrooms furnished with beds embedded in the cupboards. The bed can be folded and concealed to allow for extra living space in the day. The apartment is entirely conceived to open towards the exterior. Nonetheless, the use of large sliding doors allows a creation of intimacy when necessary.

LEFT AND NEXT
The kitchen is completely separated from the rest. However, the glass sliding door allows a view of the sea. Horizontal groove lines on the MDF panels are consistent throughout the apartment.

LEFT
Cabinets in MDF, ribbed and painted white: knobs are exclusively from a limited range for boats.

Parquet in bleached oak; shelves and tables are in oak wood. On the ceiling, directional spotlights are integrated; on the right of the cupboard are spotlights embedded in the floor.

20 GREAT RESORTS

CONTEMPORARY INTERIOR OF A CAMPINE FARM

A campine farm, designed by Vlassak-Verhulst, is redesigned by Christel De Vos and Bjorn Van Tornbout (Sphere) in a contemporary style.

The interior of this residence situated in the countryside maintains a close relation with its natural surroundings. It reveals, in a whole, a sentiment filled with space, serenity and conviviality.

The kitchen is designed after a glasshouse. A large table in oak (Sphere) and LLoyd Loom chairs are by Vincent Sheppard. Tap from Dornbracht.

LEFT

In the kitchen space, old bluestone is installed on the floor. The kitchen block is made of solid oak with the worktop in volcanic stone (Obumex). MDF board partition. All switches are from Ticino. The wrought iron door is custom-made. Lighting is from Modular.

P.118-119

Table décor by Gunther Lambert. The tablecloth and blinds are in linen.

P.120-121

On the left of the photo, two photophore-like candle holders resting on oak blocks are by Gunther Lambert. The blinds are controlled by an automation system. The air-conditioning and heater are also integrated in the project. The heater is integrated in the floor under large oak strips.

In the master bedroom, varnished parquet is installed on the floor. A bed from Treca; side tables in ebony wood.

The children bedroom's is in blue with Treca bed and Donaldson cushions.

The baby's room, with a white cabinet from Flamant.

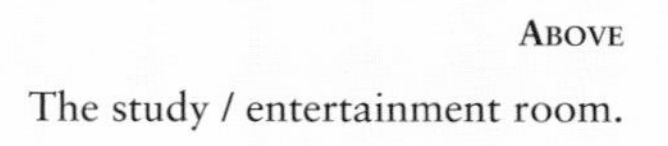

Above

The study / entertainment room.

The bathroom is in Carrara marble. Bath linen from Scapa.

On the foreground, two Le Corbusier armchairs in black leather. Lighting from Modular. Oak parquet in large strips.

Next

The studio in tints of grey and white is entirely custom-made by Stuyts.

Right

This basin cabinet finished in Winckelmans mosaic is a twinkle of the remote past and a rural characteristic of the house. The walls are finished in a washable paint lightly textured in tobacco colour.

The construction of roof in timber in the night room on the mezzanine is lightly sanded and treated with light grey patina that highlights and preserves the original colours of wood. The curved railing is in harmony with the staircase in patinated solid old oak. Flexible and equipped with a dimming function, the bronze study lamps by Stephane Davidts function to your wishes. All new bed linen trends are presented at Lacra Lifestyle.

Left

The bathroom is finished in small horizontal tiles, Kronos Brick, which are in harmony with the style of the basin and visually enlarge the space. Bath linen and other accessories in warm colours and contrasting materials soften the austere lines of the bathroom furniture. Textile and accessories are available at Lacra Lifestyle.

A TIMELESS AND CURRENT ART OF LIVING

Flamant Home Interiors is a Belgian enterprise that has, in a short time, become an international brand in interior design.

Flamant owes its success mainly to the concept of shops dedicated to habitat that the enterprise has launched on the prestigious commercial roads in Brussels, Antwerp, Knokke-le-Zoute, Gand, Liege, Hasselt, Paris, Lille, Breda, Hambourg, etc.

Flamant is known for its timeless classical style with contemporary accents.

LEFT AND ABOVE

A classical interior with some contemporary accents. A Verone coffee table and an Alabama armchair in dark grey denim. Two walls plates and Carolina candle holders with base.

Lars dining chairs surround a Jermond table. A William cabinet and a white Martine lamp.

A Rennes table and a sideboard with three compartments. Treviso ceiling light.

A Preston coffee table. A Columbia sofa in natural linen. A Gasmere natural plaid.

A Columbia sofa in unbleached linen.

CONTEMPORARY TRANSFORMATION OF A COUNTRY HOUSE IN WALLOON BRABANT

A house, designed in 1970 by architect Librecht, was purchased, entirely reviewed and transformed in 2002 by its current owners (a couple with three children). In this exceptional country house, Instore was given carte blanche for the interior design.

The openness of space and search for perspectives have presided the conception for the interior realised by this Brussels architectural office. The homogeneity of materials and colours has allowed the creation of a purified serene ambience.

All elements of design were specially conceived for this exclusive residence: door handles and furniture, bathroom accessories, custom-made furniture, etc. The ensemble is equipped with a very sophisticated home automation system. The grey oak flooring is treated; all custom-made furniture in grey sanded oak are also treated.

LEFT AND ABOVE
The creation of a sentiment of space and perspectives presides this project of Instore office.

NEXT
The Charles living room ensemble is from B&B Italia. SMCH chaises longues from Maxalto. The leather artworks are from Frederique Hoet – Segers and Jumping Bull.

LEFT AND ABOVE
A Dumbo table and the Brigitta chairs are from Promemoria. The Charles bench is from B&B Italia.

NEXT
Above the Marcel B&B Italia sofa is a painting by Sophie Cauvin. The Cantena coffee table is from Casamilano, the Minerale carpet is from Danskina.

Pierre / Paul lighting from Ingomaurer. The bench in MDF Italia is conceived by Xavier Lust.

The CITE armchair from Vitra is created by Jean Prouve. A pouf from Paola Lenti.

NEXT
The bathtub, basins and tap fittings are from Boffi.

Frank table and Caffe chairs are from Promemoria. The lighting is from Fontana Arte. The photo on the left known as "Lost Paradise" is by Marie-Jo Lafontaine.

A lounge chair by Charles Eames for Vitra.

"Tulip" chair designed by Eero Saarinen.

LEFT
A WK6 Boffi kitchen.

ART AND DESIGN IN A COUNTRY HOUSE

A couple passionate about contemporary art requested interior designer Marc Stellamans to design their country house, which was constructed in 1985.

Almost 20 years later, this interior remains surprisingly current: modern art and furniture design form a perfect symbiosis without destroying the convivial characteristics and warmth of this modern country house.

All the walls are finished in painted fabric. The colours of natural stone, flooring and parquet are in perfect harmony: Massangis Clair tiles and flooring in grey treated oak.

The television corner with a Nigel Hall painting on the left foreground. Flooring in grey treated oak.

NEXT
The living room close to the study area is furnished with armchairs and table from B&B Italia and a woven carpet of Bathlolmeus from Torhout. Fabrics are from Bayard and Boirond.

LEFT
The black painting is by Pierre Soulages.

WIDE
WHITE
SPACE

A SERENE UNIVERSE FOR A UNIQUE FURNITURE DESIGN COLLECTION

In an apartment building designed by architect Marc Corbiau, Vincent Van Duysen, also an architect, has designed a duplex that houses a fascinating collection of furniture design from the 20th century, of which some are original pieces by Jean-Michel Frank, Charles & Ray Eames for Vitra, Knoll etc.

Vincent Van Duysen worked with solid materials to conserve the neutrality and geometry of the ensemble: Statuario Carrara marble in large panels for floor and wall finishes, and tinted oak with purified lines conceived by Van Duysen. The black and white contrast creates a superb confrontation and accentuates the place where each piece of furniture occupies in this extremely sober and serene interior.

LEFT AND ABOVE
The living room with chairs by Charles & Ray Eames and an armchair by Jean-Michel Frank. The low table in lacquered aluminium is conceived by architect Van Duysen.

NEXT
Coherent use of Statuario Carrara marble on the floor and walls contributes in a large quantity, a sense of uniformity, spatial and purity of this interior. The diptych above the sofa is by Italian photographer Massimo Vitali.

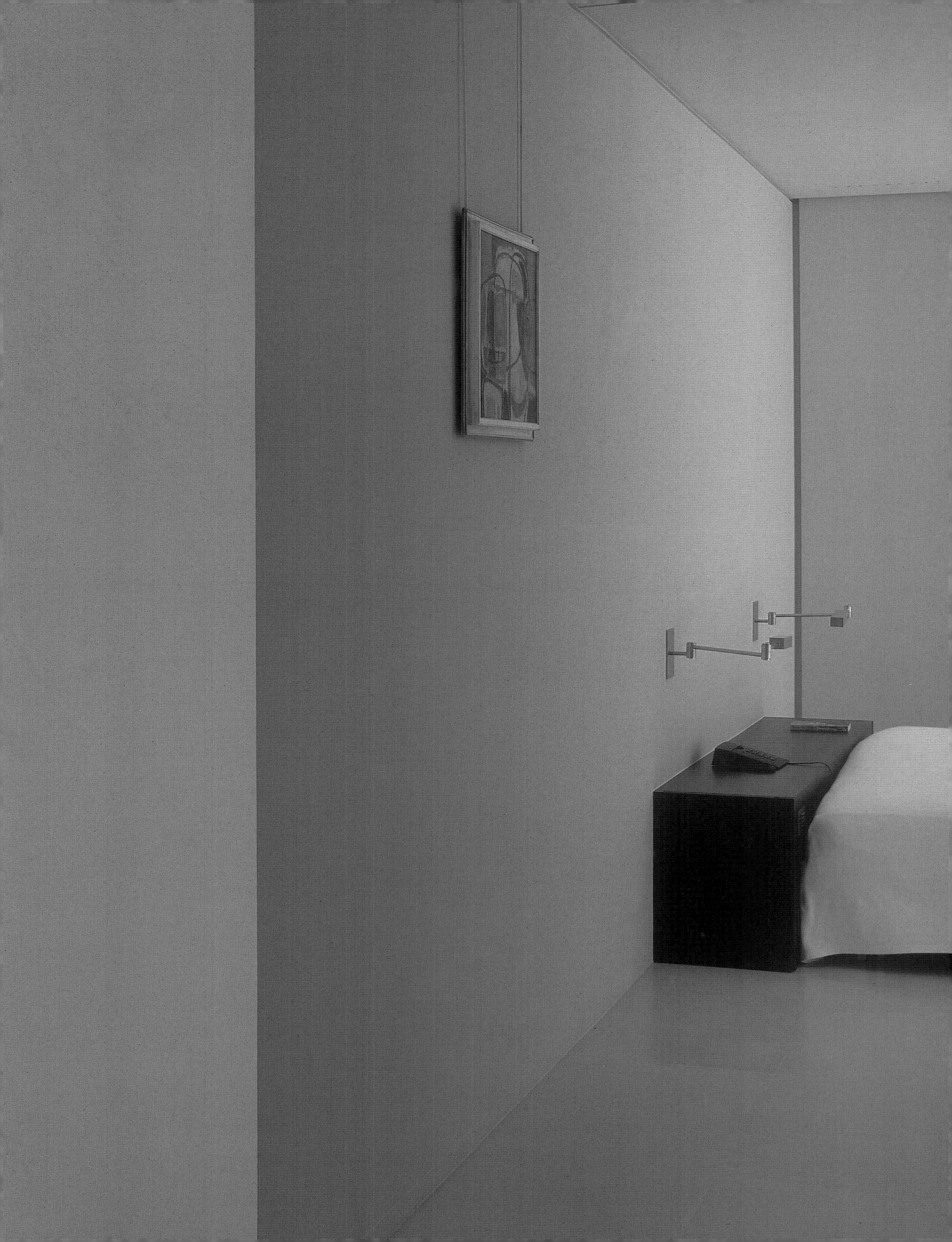

The door-high headboard is finished in mole-coloured wool. Bed, side table and bed spread are designed by the architect. The furniture is made of glass and lacquered wood. The woollen bedspread is in two shades of red.

A monochromatic palette of colour in the bathroom.

NEW SPACE FOR A UNIQUE COLLECTION OF CONTEMPORARY ART

Philip Simoen has transformed the stale interior of a 1985 villa into a pleasant living place where a beautiful space is reserved for a unique collection of contemporary art.

On the structural plan, few elements are modified in the residence: only a large partition of the chimney is demolished and on top of that, Simoen has created a secondary window opening in the living room, which offers a view of the garden. In this manner, the occupants take full advantage of the art pieces placed in the garden: a vase by Allan McCollum, a structure of Sol Lewitt, a collection of statues of Richard Deacon and an artwork by Anisg Kapoor.

LEFT AND ABOVE
The living room is furnished with armchairs from B&B Italia. The television and hi-fi equipment cabinet next to the chimney is designed by Philip Simoen. The large strips of oak flooring are in a greyish brown tint. Lighting from Delta Light.

The painting above the chimney is by Karel Appel. The objects on the coffee table are by Sol Lewitt. A painting by Richter and an object by Jan Vercruysse.

The living room is furnished with sofa and armchairs by Christian Liaigre. On the right of the photo shows the new opening into the garden.

A view of the hall where the floor is finished in made-to-measure volcanic stone.

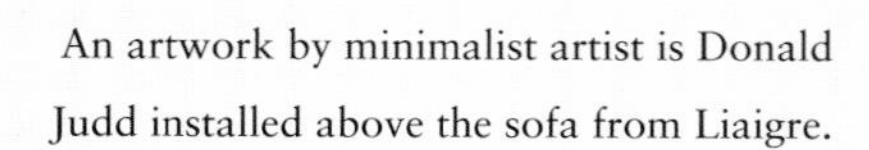

An artwork by minimalist artist is Donald Judd installed above the sofa from Liaigre.

The dining table constitutes of a sanded Carrara marble slab. Leather chairs by Poul Kjaerholm. The yellow painting is by Robert Mangold.

The piano corner.

LEFT AND ABOVE

Kitchen floor and worktop are in Buxy stone in greyish yellow shades. The table is in sanded oak and the chairs are from Maxalto. Kitchen cabinets in satin lacquer are designed by Philip Simoen and realised by Wilfra. Appliances from Gaggenau and Smeg. The console is also created by Simoen.

P.200-203

This carpet of pebbles has a unique feel.

BIBLIOGRAPHY

Bataille & Ibens. Projets & objets 1968/2003. Ludion, 2003.

Charlotte & Peter Fiell, 1000 chairs. Taschen, 2000.

Kenneth Frampton, Modern Architecture. A critical history. Thames & Hudson, 1992.

P. Loze, Marc Corbiau, Architecte. Mardaga, 2000.

Made in Belgium Design Book. MMAP/HKRA, 2001.

Catherine McDermott, Twentieth-Century Design. Carlton Books, 1997.

John Pawson, Minimum. Phaidon, 1998.

Alberto Piovano, Vincent Van Duysen. Ed. Gustavo Gili, 2001.

NEXT
Kitchen by Instore.
Bathtub and basins
from Boffi (Ifiumi) and
tap fittings from
Minimal, also by Boffi.

PHOTOGRAPHY CREDITS

All the photos: Jo Pauwels with the exception of:

P. 116-129	Patrick Verbeeck
P. 136-139	Flamant Home Interiors
P. 166-179	Jean-Luc Laloux
P. 222-223	Jean-Luc Laloux